IX CHEL WISDOM

7 Teachings from the Mayan Sacred Feminine

SHONAGH HOME

LOGOSOPHIA LLC

Logosophia LLC
90 Oteen Church Road
Asheville, NC 28805
https://logosophiabooks.com
logosophiabooks@gmail.com

ISBN: 978-1-7350432-5-8

Cover design by Magrit Baurecht
https://corecreativeteam.com

Printed in the United States of America

10 9 8 7 6 5 4 3 2 1

PRAISE FOR IX CHEL WISDOM

"If you open Ix Chel Wisdom *a crack, you will hear the whisper of women sighing and singing. If you dare to read it, you will be swept up in an astonishing inner adventure that will empower you deeply. The Wise Woman Way spirals in these messages. The words of the Grandmother's song echo in Shonagh's words. The cloak of the Ancients is being rewoven with sturdy threads such as these. Join hands with the circle of women!"*

~ Susun S. Weed, author of *New Menopausal Years the Wise Woman Way*

"I absolutely love the way Shonagh brings home the message that being female is so much more than the stereotypical surface images we receive in our culture. The reason why this book is so powerful is because it ties all of us to the ancient wisdom passed down by a lineage of strong and loving grandmothers, dating back to Mayan civilization. Shonagh brings those messages to life for us in this century, when we so badly need to embrace our beautiful femininity.

"Can you imagine how much our world would be transformed, if we women truly learn to value ourselves and our bodies at a deep, magical level? By following the principles in Shonagh's book, we can — one step at a time.

"For me, this is the paragraph that sums up Shonagh's work so well: 'The evolved feminine walks the path of beauty. She regards herself and all life as sacred. She is sovereign unto herself — she's not enslaved or anyone's fool. She relies upon her intuition and wisdom. She is connected directly to Source and is aware of her connection to all things above and below. She seeks the truth and

embodies wisdom, healing, and service to the Divine. Expression and expansion of the energies that honor all life are found within her. This is the feminine I hope to see expressed around the world. She is sorely needed at this time.'

"I want some of that! If you do, too, please read this book."

~ Janet Luhrs, author of *The Simple Living Guide, Simple Loving*, and proprietress of www.simpleliving.com

"What a joy to read your book. I was truly touched by your journey. When you received your initiation and baptism in the cave, I felt as if I was right there with you. Your willingness to share such sacred personal moments (and others throughout the book) is a testament to your desire to empower other women. Through the teachings of Ix Chel, and your own personal experiences, you transmit, and passionately inspire us to remember, and reclaim the natural beauty of our earth-body, and the divine wisdom that dwells within every woman's heart. A rich offering to empower the spirit of women!"

~ Janis Deluca RN, Mentor and guide for women, Tantra Educator

"Shonagh weaves her personal journey and spiritual teachers with Ix Chel's transmissions beautifully. The heart of my feminine was deeply touched. I felt an awakening encouraging the Goddess in me to rise again. Read Shonagh's book and you will feel empowered, touched and healed by her words."

~ Patricia White Buffalo

"Shonagh has a beautiful way of expressing the essence of life in her writing. She helps the reader open portals that allow a new awareness and consciousness journey into the heart. Thank you Mother Ix Chel for your teachings and wise rituals. And, thank you Shonagh for being open to receiving them."

~ Kathleen Hosner, PhD, author of *Full Heart, Satisfied Belly*

DEDICATION

For my beautiful daughters,

Maddie and Serena.

And for my mother,

who always believed in me.

ACKNOWLEDGEMENTS

My deepest gratitude goes to my ex-husband, John, who helped birth this book through his undying support and encouragement.

I have been blessed to work with extraordinary spiritual teachers these past six years. I am humbled and grateful for the magnificent gifts of their teachings. My deep appreciation goes to both Miguel Angel and Don Jose, whose faith in me resulted in this book. You have both contributed great gifts to my spiritual growth and I will always love you for that. To Trudy Woodcock, your friendship and loving support through the writing of this book was a balm to my heart.

My thanks to Isabel Lambert — you have brought me to a place of grounded centeredness, which has enabled me to bring forward this book and I am grateful for your caring focus. John Knowlton, the nudge you gave me to hold that first full moon ceremony — my indebtedness to you for inspiring me to 'be big.'

Brugh Joy, you have given me a foundation of heart-centered awareness from which to work. I have been blessed to receive your wise teachings and I've shifted deeply as a result. I bow to you in gratitude.

I have expanded my consciousness exponentially because of Tom Kenyon's teachings. Tom, you have been a light on my path to the heart and I treasure every opportunity to work with you. I cannot thank you enough for all you have done for me.

My sincere thanks to the beautiful oracle and sound healer, Jennifer Posada — you have been an inspiration and a light to me. I am so very grateful for the opportunity I've had to study with you and open to my gifts.

Judi Sion, thank you for your magnificent fire. You have had a profound influence on my life.

And, Janis DeLuca, thank you for inspiring me to 'dance' the goddess!

Patricia White Buffalo, you have helped me to heal deeply. You are a master teacher and a treasure on this earth plane.

I want to thank my beloved friends, Alisa Sylling, Isabel Dunay, Sarah Pella, and Jeri LaShay for encouraging and sustaining me through this wondrous process. I am blessed beyond words to have friends like you in my life.

To the women who have attended my full moon ceremonies, your presence, your gifts, and your support have enriched my life enormously.

To my editor, Sherry Folb, I give my heartfelt thanks — your meticulous attention to detail and words of wisdom inspired me to take my writing to the next level.

Magrit Baurecht — thank you for taking my dream and manifesting it so beautifully when creating the cover and interior for this book.

Lastly, thank you Ix Chel, Mother of my Heart — I am full and radiant with your love. Thank you grandmother Ix Mukane, Heart of the Earth — you come to me every time I call you. Thank you Mama Mary for holding me close. My heart is full. The goddess lives. A showering of blessings to all!

TABLE OF CONTENTS

Foreword | 1

Now It Is The Woman Who Has The Torch | 7

Introduction | 11

Ceremony and the Power of the Circle | 23

TRANSMISSION I | The Magic of the Womb | 37

My Thoughts Transmission I | 41

TRANSMISSION II | Sacred Bathing | 47

My Thoughts Transmission II | 51

TRANSMISSION III | Beauty | 57

My Thoughts Transmission III | 61

TRANSMISSION IV | Spaciousness and Creating | 67

My Thoughts Transmission IV | 71

TRANSMISSION V | Radiance of the Sun | 79

My Thoughts Transmission V | 84

TRANSMISSION VI | Path of the Heart | 89

My Thoughts Transmission VI | 93

TRANSMISSION VII | Sacred Blood | 99

My Thoughts Transmission VII | 104

Reflections on the Teachings of Ix Chel | 109

About the Author | 115

Helpful Books and Websites | 117

Foreword

When my dear friend Shonagh emailed me to tell me she was writing a book about Ix Chel and the Mayan Sacred Feminine, I had no doubt that she would do it and do it well. She is a woman of power and she inspires that kind of faith. Reading the first draft moved me deeply and brought to the surface my early experiences with the Maya Goddess Ix Chel.

Like Shonagh, I was first introduced to her through my teacher, Miguel Angel Vergara, and I, too, felt the need to write down the messages received during my morning meditations. I call these writings my conversations with Ix Chel. Through these conversations I came to remember, recognize, and accept the perfect spiritual being that I am. Even more exciting, along with this insight came the ability to see this perfection in everyone I meet. There is no separation — we are clearly ONE.

Of course this was just the beginning. Ix Chel then introduced me to Ix Mukane, the grandmother and Heart of the Earth. This took place at the sacred Maya site of Tikal, in Guatemala, while with a group led by Miguel Angel. The form was a dramatic out of body journey to the Heart of the Earth where I had a personal audience with Ix Mukane. Her message was clear and simple, *"Now is the time to awaken. Ask me for what you need. I am listening and I will give it to you."* In that instant life changed for me. I knew my purpose was to continue my awakening process and help guide others on their path of awareness. I knew I would receive what I needed in order to continue.

Each month I host a Maya Full Moon ceremony at my home in Mérida, Yucatán. A group of women join me in the circle to connect with the energy of the Full Moon, honor Ix Chel, and share our experiences as we move along our spiritual path. It is one of the most fulfilling and rewarding things I have ever done. With each new ceremony, with each new woman who joins us, with each full moon visit with Ix Chel, we can feel the awakening of the Sacred Feminine.

An important part of the awakening is the awareness that we are now Adult Children and it is time for us to take responsibility for the care of our Mother Earth. It is not surprising that we are awakening to this consciousness now when many of us are faced with the care of elderly parents on a personal level.

We are in the same situation with our inner Mother, Ix Chel. She has sustained us, loved us, and nurtured us throughout the ages and now it is our turn, as her Adult Children, to give something back. Raising the Sacred Feminine to balance with the Sacred Masculine is one thing we can do that will truly make a difference.

When I asked Ix Chel to lead me to what I needed to do she answered, *"I am in your heart. You are my eyes, ears, my hands, my arms and legs. Follow your heart. I am in everything you do."*

Ix Chel is in each and every one of us and in everything we do. When I see people like Shonagh step up and do what needs to be done, I have great faith in the future. We each have a role in the creation of the evolving new world and I am sure Shonagh would join me in inviting you to discover what your contribution might be and then just go ahead and do it. Now is the time. You are not alone. Do it now.

"In Lak Ech"
Trudy Woodcock

Now it is the Woman who has the Torch

Oh, Powerful Lady…

Oh, Lady of the Flame…

Oh, Lady of the Two Worlds…

Oh, Lady, well beloved of the Father…

Arise now to the Divine Warrior

To the Lady of the Power and the Force

To the Blessed Mother Ix Chel, Ix Mukane,
Maria, Shakti, to the Sacred Feminine

The Eternal Feminine; As Above So Below

She is the Primordial Force that sustains the
Gods and Men!

Miguel Angel Vergara Calleros
www.casakin.org

Introduction

Everyone is buzzing about the Mayan calendar, which ends in 2012. Even Hollywood has gotten its greedy hands on the subject. Despite this obsession with the mysterious Maya, almost nothing is being said about the Mayan Sacred Feminine.

The Maya have their own holy mother whom they call Ix Chel — pronounced 'eeshel.' Ix Chel is the goddess of the earth, the moon, all fluids, fertility, healing, and healing plants. She is also known as 'Rainbow Mother.' Ix Chel is shown as an old woman holding a pot in her hands. On her head is a coiled up snake, a symbol of the kundalini that has risen through her body and resides on her crown chakra. She is powerful, benevolent, playful, and nurturing.

I first learned about Ix Chel when I accompanied my husband, John, on a tour of the sacred sites of the Maya in 2006. John had been fascinated with all things Mayan, including the Mayan Calendar and its mysterious completion in 2012. Initially, I did not feel drawn to the Mayan culture but I gladly accompanied him for the adventure. John and I have always been voracious spiritual students. Often, one of us feels drawn to a book or a teacher and it is the other partner who ends up enhanced by the discovery. So, we seem to lead each other into wondrous directions we wouldn't necessarily follow if we were on our own.

Our journey in 2006 was part of a group tour we'd signed up for with a teacher from Europe. As fate would have it, we had the unexpected pleasure of meeting two people who would change our lives dramatically. Trudy Woodcock of Iluminado Tours was the person in charge of our tour and her teacher, Miguel Angel Vergara, was our shaman/guide. As the four of us spent more time together during the trip — we realized that we all felt a connection and an enduring friendship ensued.

Miguel Angel is one of those teachers who speaks from his heart. He has an incredible depth of knowledge about the Mayan Sacred Feminine. We were graced to attend a talk Miguel gave on the Mayan Goddesses. I wanted to learn more about them as I have always resonated with the divine feminine in her many forms. I learned about Ix Chel and also grandmother Ix Mukane — pronounced 'eesh moo kanay' — who resides in the center of the earth. The temples at Uxmal carry a very feminine energy. Some Mayan spiritual teachers consider it to be a place where the divine feminine energy is strongest on the planet.

We visited many Mayan sites during the tour and had the privilege of lingering long enough to wander through the temple remains and become sensitized to the energies there. I walked alone through different sections of the temples where I would feel called to do vocal toning as a way of offering my appreciation and love to the Spirits. It was at the temples of Uxmal where I was stunned to receive a showering of deep love and appreciation back. It moved me to tears and my reverence for the Spirits of those sacred places was immensely deepened. I had no doubt that I had spent lifetimes in those temples. I knew I would have to come back someday and I felt my work was just beginning.

WAITING TO CONTINUE

Two years went by, during which time I continued my intensive spiritual study with teachers, Tom Kenyon, Isabel Lambert, Brugh Joy, and John Knowlton. From the age of 40, I have had a burning desire to deepen my connection with Spirit and expand my consciousness. I've been dearly blessed to have been guided to teachers who are both highly evolved spiritually and also blessedly human with great wit and accessibility. Miguel Angel is no exception and several times I talked about returning to work with him but the timing was always off.

In May of 2009, I had planned to fly to Peru with my teacher, John Knowlton, a shaman. We were to spend three weeks climbing sacred mountains and doing ceremonial work with the Peruvian shamans; however, a couple of months before the trip Knowlton decided to postpone going until the following year. I believe when one door closes, another door opens. So my initial disappointment faded as the thought of flying to the Yucatan to work with Miguel again came to mind. I had a feeling this was meant to be all along. My email inquiry to Trudy was answered immediately with an affirmative, "Yes! Miguel would love to work with you one-on-one. Just let me know which week you'd like to fly down." I love the way life works.

TRANSFORMATION OF CONSCIOUSNESS

And so began a profound transformation of my consciousness that has colored every aspect of my life.

During my week long stay in the Yucatan, Miguel worked with me daily, teaching me ceremony, meditation to bring through wisdom, and Mayan mystery teachings passed down from his teacher. He informed me that he would be taking me to the sacred cave of the Maya next to the temples of Uxmal on Wednesday. We would be meeting a shaman named Don Jose, who works with the 'alluxes' or Spirits of the cave.

On Wednesday morning, we made the drive and met with Don Jose. The timing for this was excellent as I had flown to Mexico during the swine flu scare and there wasn't a tourist to be found. As a result, we had the cave to ourselves without any tourists breaking the energy of the work Don Jose would be doing.

At the entrance to the cave Don Jose and Miguel Angel stood on either side of me. Don Jose spoke no English and Miguel was there to translate for him and support the work. Before entering, Don Jose asked me if I had a wish I would like granted. I responded that it was my hope to go back home and be a powerful teacher/healer to empower others to expand their consciousness and discover their true divinity. Don Jose smiled and said, "There is more." I was a bit taken aback and said simply that my whole intention with all of this work was to deepen my own connection to Spirit. That was my prayer. Don Jose looked very serious and said, "You will receive a Mayan baptism."

MY MAYAN BAPTISM

At that moment I didn't know that he had only baptized people a handful of times in all the years he has been a shaman — which I learned later from Trudy. What I did know was that I was entering a portal of sorts — it's a feeling I get when I'm about to experience something very rare and special.

Entering the caves was like stepping into the quiet stillness of an ancient temple. Everywhere, there were amazing protrusions of stalactites that didn't look real. We could have been on another planet it was so otherworldly. There were little bats hanging from the ceiling and occasionally one would flit by, perhaps curious by our presence.

As we walked deeper into the cave, Don Jose showed me a stalactite suspended from the ceiling that was releasing drops of water onto a stalagmite directly below. The top of the lower stalagmite had been shaped over time into a depression, like a bowl, to capture each drop of water. To the Mayans, this is the most sacred fluid of all. It contains 'itz' which is considered to be a direct gift and blessing from the Spirits. Itz is an essence or liquid like semen, dew, or tears. The most sacred and revered of all is the dripping water inside a cave. It was this water that Don Jose used to clear and open my chakras. Further into the cave, there was a second hidden 'bowl' of itz water that Don Jose used for my baptism.

Before the baptism, I was taken to a place in the cave to be formally introduced to the Mayan holy mother, Ix Chel. Don Jose pointed to a ledge across from us and told me to focus on that place. I am not clairvoyant but I have a highly developed sense of feeling called 'clairsentience.' I could feel Ix Chel standing across from me with countless Mayans surrounding her. I felt her eyes looking deeply into mine and the connection to her was sealed when Don Jose got very excited and exclaimed that Ix Chel came into my heart. I felt a tremendous peace and calm inside. He looked surprised, excited, and extremely pleased. "Now you are ready for your baptism," he said.

The baptism was beautiful — quiet and reverent. Don Jose used more of the sacred water to anoint my body and I felt waves of emotion throughout my being. I knew this was a pivotal moment. I knew then, that when I walked out of that cave, I would be forever transformed.

When the baptism was finished, they took me to the farthest part of the cave where the ceiling was very high. There were two large holes in the ceiling with sunlight streaming through casting rays of luminous light into the cave below. Flying in a vortex pattern through the rays were hundreds of swallows swooping and singing delightfully. It was a most extraordinary sight. It seemed as if they were dancing in the air and I could have spent the rest of the afternoon basking in the energy of that enchanted, holy place.

After the ceremony in the caves I had lunch with Trudy and Miguel. I started to tell Miguel how touched I was by what had happened and I had to stop as I could feel tears of emotion welling up inside me. Miguel just nodded. There was no need for words. We were speaking from our hearts.

Later that day when I was back in the city of Merida exploring the streets, I suddenly realized that I could feel into the hearts of the people on the sidewalk around me. It was so intimate and beautiful and immense that I began to weep. I made my way back to my hotel room and stayed by myself for the rest of the evening to integrate my experiences in the cave. Clearly, I had been opened and it was important for me to be alone with that and do some meditating and journaling to ground myself.

MY FIRST TRANSMISSION

In one of my meditation experiences that evening, I had an image of Ix Chel stretching my neck so that my head was high off the ground. She was telling me to hold my head high, to be proud, and walk with honor and integrity. I was thinking about that when words came in that I knew were from her and I began writing until they stopped. My first transmission from Ix Chel was this:

"The people will come. They always come when you bring the truth and light. They will flock to you, child. Hear my words. I speak to you now as you write. I am in your heart now forever. You will not lose me. Study your books. Play with your rituals. Have fun. Listen and look for the devas — they will help you. They are waiting to help. You are in training and you are learning well. We love your attitude and we feel the intensity of your desire. Just relax into it for the unfolding has begun and there is no end to the levels of opening you will experience. You can change the world. It is a combination of energies. It is very powerful. The power of women gathered to seed the world with light. In Lak Ech."

After this transmission I saw myself leading full moon ceremonies at my home. I knew I was to bring the offerings of Ix Chel to the women in my part of the world. Her message was clear. She would always be with me. It was up to me to call on her to bring a teaching through that would benefit me and everyone else who felt drawn to her.

I've never imagined myself to be a channel. I have been clairsentient since I was a child. I have always been able to 'feel' Spirits and 'feel' messages. I also have clair-cognition, which is instant knowing. As a child I had no knowledge of what that was so I simply called it 'confirmations.' I knew that when certain information came in — that was that. There was no bargaining or trying to change it. It was the final word. I always trusted that communication because it was always right.

What I am experiencing with these transmissions from Ix Chel is simply tuning into her energy. I begin by sitting quietly and call gently to her and wait for what is usually a rush of words that come into me. I write until the words subside. When finished I look to see what I've received. I find the process deeply humbling and I'm filled with gratitude when given a message from her. In my meditations I often visualize myself running into her arms to hug and kiss her. Ix Chel lives in my heart. In fact, she calls herself 'mother of my heart.' She is dear to me and it is with great reverence and humility that I present these offerings to all who feel called.

Ceremony
and the Power
of the Circle

During my stay in the Yucatan, it became clear to me that I was to begin holding full moon ceremonies for women. Ix Chel came into my awareness to say that if I held these ceremonies at my home, she would come through with a teaching for me to pass on to the women attending. I felt that she wanted me to introduce her energy to the women in my area so they would become aware of the power and magic of the Mayan Cosmic Mother.

My friend, Trudy, inspired me to host these types of ceremonies since she had been hosting them at her home for several months. She would invite women to come and connect with each other through the honoring of the full moon energies. She said this was a wonderful way to create community and use the power of the group to affect change both personally and collectively.

I made a plan to hold my first full moon ceremony in July of 2009. When I mentioned this to my teacher, John Knowlton, he urged me to do it in June. John felt I was fully ready to step into this, assuring me that those who felt called to participate would come. Now I really had to do it and there was no stalling.

The week before the full moon, I sat naked in the sunshine, basking in the rays, and writing in my journal. I thought this might be a good time to call in Rainbow

Mother Ix Chel, so I closed my eyes and tuned into her. As soon as I felt a rush of words coming in I began to write. When I read the passage I'd written I felt chills go down my body. It was about the magic of the womb and I knew instantly I had connected to an ancient, matriarchal teaching.

The following day, I sent an e-mail to all the women I thought might be interested in coming to a full moon ceremony. I explained that we'd be doing a fire ceremony and that fire is a great transformer. I asked everyone to bring two offerings. The first offering was a written intention of something they would like to release in their life. The second offering would be a written intention of something they would like to create. I wrote that I also had a transmission from Ix Chel and I explained who she was. I wisely requested an RSVP so I could prepare accordingly. I expected an intimate group of 4 or 5 women. I was floored when I received 22 emails accepting my invitation.

We have a forest in the back of our property and we had recently created a circular clearing with a fire pit in the center. I had to extend the perimeter of the circle to accommodate all of these women. I had a distinct sense that something big was happening. The letters of response were so effusive. Women had written things like, "This is the perfect thing for me right now." and, "Bless you for doing this. You have no idea how much I need this!" I was genuinely shocked and at the same time, I felt it was a clear message from Ix Chel telling me — the time is NOW.

THE FIRST CEREMONY

That first ceremony ended up with 17 attendees. Those who couldn't make it actually emailed or phoned me rather than doing a no-show. They wanted to make sure they would be invited to the next ceremony. I was becoming increasingly aware of how hungry women were for this kind of experience.

The ceremony itself was beautiful. I began with a prayer in Mayan, asking for permission to open the portals. I then opened the directions and invited the women to bring in any deities, angels, or loved ones they wished to have support them and share the space. When we began the fire ceremony, we made our offerings in silence. I felt at the time that it should be between each individual woman, the fire elemental, and her inner guides and teachers.

Observing the offerings going into the fire, I was deeply touched by the level of care each woman had taken in composing her offerings. There is a saying that goes, "The face you show is the face you get back." These women had shown up with reverence and integrity and I realized in that moment just how very important this ceremony was for all of us.

The next few days I received many letters of thanks from the women who'd participated.

Here is just a sampling of the responses:

- "Thank you for offering your most beautiful self to all of us. You are a GIFT and your ceremony was bliss!"

- "I am amazed by the rich circle of women you have drawn together."

- "My goodness, you are so fabulous, so fully expansive, brilliant, and shining. You are a wonderful example to us all of living our power. It was generous to create the sacred space, the social space, and to share the wealth of love and light that flows so magnificently through you. I'm filled with awe and gratitude. I know that you've begun something and I'm blessed to witness and participate."

- "Thank you so much. I had a smile on my face all evening, and then some interesting dreams. What a beautiful thing it was."

- "What an amazing group of women you brought together through your wonderful energy. Thank you for this beautiful evening. I am still processing all that happened. I bless you for the powerful Spirit that you are on the earth plane."

This was not a coincidence as the following month 22 women attended the full moon ceremony. And the letters of thanks continued to pour in. What is it about gathering in ceremony that feels so primary to so many people? What happens to us when we gather in this way? The following is my attempt to understand and explain this ancient practice and hopefully inspire women to create something like this for themselves.

THE POWER OF THE CIRCLE

Groups have gathered together in circle for millennia. It is a symbol of wholeness and integration. When in circle, all are considered equal. The center of the circle is the place of Spirit. When we gather in circle we are in the energy of unity, which creates a vortex of power that emanates from the group. Thought, action, mind, and body are united in circle. There is no beginning and no end, only an expanded group consciousness that magnifies the power of the whole. Holding hands offers a deepening of our relationship to each other as we are now physically connected rather than standing alone. Healing on every level is possible by gathering in circle.

ABOUT CEREMONY

Ceremony is a means of bringing energy into our intentions. Whether we want to honor a rite of passage, give thanks, seek guidance, or any other intention — this is an effective way to do so. In the deep psyche there is no difference between what's real and what's imagined. The psyche responds to our thoughts and experiences both externally and internally. When we are involved in ceremony we are participating in an event that has been created with the integrity of intention.

Ceremonies are customarily broken up into three sections. The beginning of each ceremony always starts with some type of invocation. Often the Spirits of the directions or certain deities are called in to support the event. If you are particularly sensitive, you will feel a shift in the energy of the circle after this is done. These are very real energies and they will be present to radiate their essence. This also establishes the sacredness of the space and the work, which will be done there. It creates a shift from the normal, day-to-day activities, to a focused reverence for the intention at hand.

The body of the ceremony is the longest in duration. This is what you've gathered for and it is deeply meaningful. There are many ceremonies we can follow that have been passed down by the elders of various cultures. We can also create something unique. Always remember that we are powerful Spirits/Humans and we have the ability to create our own rituals in whatever way feels sacred to us.

The final part is the closing. It is important to thank and release the forces you have called in to support the ceremony. All participants need to have closure so they can release the experience and shift back to their individual lives. It is also nice to have each participant offer a word or a prayer in ending.

TIMING

The ancients held their ceremonies at specific times of the year in order to glean all they could from the energetic forces of nature and Spirit. They understood that everything was connected. With this understanding, they aligned themselves with the placement of the planets or the seasonal turning points like the solstices and equinoxes. This brought the heightened energies of these natural occurrences into their rituals, giving them much more power. It also connected them deeply to the universal cycles of the earth and the cosmos.

The new moon represents the birth of the moon's cycles. Seeds planted by the ancients were put into the soil at the time of the new moon. Engaging in ceremony at this moon phase accesses the energies needed to support the seeding of our intentions. As the moon grows fuller, our intentions are nurtured so they can draw strength from that support and come into manifestation, in harmony with universal flow.

The full moon has always been a powerful time to gather for ceremony. Cultures have been doing so since the dawn of man. The full moon represents the completion of cycles. It's a good time to release what no longer serves or celebrate the completion of something one has begun. It's also a time when darkness is illuminated, creating an opportunity to take stock of what needs to be addressed or brought forward. It is a wonderful time to gather and join in song and dance under the moon's light. Honoring the moon monthly keeps us in rhythm with the natural cycles of life.

The timing of ceremonies can also be about the changing points in people's lives — the birth of a baby, coming of age, marriage, and death. These ceremonies stress the importance of each stage of life. Through the power of ceremony, one experiences a deeper appreciation for the new stage they are in. This tunes us in to the flow of life and accentuates the gifts each phase offers.

THE POWER OF GROUP MEDITATION

A wonderful thing to incorporate into the body of the ceremony is a meditation. You can do a guided meditation or choose a theme or intention and have everyone focus on that. Group meditation is very powerful. When people come together to meditate on a common theme, a phenomenon is created called 'the maharishi effect.' This is a coherence of the consciousness of a group. It carries combined fields of intention.

Each of us has a field of energy around us known as an aura or energy field. Physicists are familiar with the electromagnetic field and the gravitational field. They are also aware of our aura, which they call the energy field. Our energy field sends waves of consciousness throughout the entire cosmos. Throw a stone into a pool of water and observe the waves emanating from it. The entire pool of water is affected in some form. In the same way, what we put out through our thoughts and actions has far-reaching effects throughout the universe.

Put a group of people together and have them meditate with a specific intention and you create in essence a 'super field' that is magnified by the number of participants. One person's energy field radiates to a certain degree. When you add a second person and they focus on a shared intention, the field grows exponentially. Keep adding more people and the field becomes huge.

It has been scientifically documented that when large groups of people meditate, the reduction of their stress levels creates a powerful sense of harmony that radiates from the group dynamic out into the environment around them. Think about the far-reaching effects of groups of people gathering all over the world to envision a world of peace, harmony, transparency, and integrity. Think of the power of our children, who have none of the blocks we adults have, gathering in groups and putting their minds together to create this. The possibilities are endless and the potential to change the face of the planet we live on is very real. Ceremony gives us a vehicle to create great change not only in our personal lives, but also in the collective and for our beautiful planet.

FINAL THOUGHTS

What an extraordinary gift to discover ceremony at this time. It is hard to imagine that just a few centuries ago many women would have been persecuted for gathering in such a way. In the middle ages it was considered heretical to think one had the authority to gather and commune with the higher realms.

Ix Chel has taught me that by gathering and claiming our birthright to personal power and direct counsel with Spirit, we send a ripple through the time/space continuum, healing the wounds of injustice our sisters from the past endured, and paving the way as models for our modern-day sisters and daughters. We teach them that by gathering with sacred purpose and intent, we access incredible wisdom and intuition, deepening our connection to each other and our Mother Earth. We are not bound by the current culture's version of woman, who is valued primarily as youthful, thin, and sexy. Through ceremony, we see deeply into each other's soul, valuing the depth of heart and wisdom each woman carries.

When we join in circle under the fullness of the moon, we increase our capacity for healing, for connection to the rhythms of life, for connection to our higher selves, and for the creation of the kind of change most people think is impossible.

The Magic of the Womb

Rainbow mother, Ix Chel, please speak to me. If you have a message for the women attending this full moon ceremony, I would very much like to give it to them.

"I am underfoot. I am all around. I am above you. I call to you now. My healing waters fill your wombs, sprouting the seeds of joy you will birth.

"Think of your wombs as temples of creation. They are more than just wombs for physical manifestation. Within a woman's womb is held the energy of creation of all things. Do not take this lightly. Utilize the energy of creation and manifestation within your womb. Think of what you wish to birth in this life, what you wish to birth on this planet. Think of this intention as a seed and place it in your womb. Then love and nurture your body as you would if you were pregnant with a child. Put your hands on your belly. Send it your adoration. Nurture this great gift you are gestating for yourself and the planet.

"Choose the time of birth. Center in yourself and you will receive the right time. Mark it on your calendar and prepare to birth it. When

the time comes, go to a sacred place, squat down, and give birth to this manifestation of beauty you have created. Send it into the earth. I am the Divine Mother Earth. I will be your midwife. Send it deep into my center, the heart of the earth. Ix Mukane, the grandmother, will receive it.

"Then rest and open to receive all the love from the Great Mother. There is profound healing and profound wisdom in this gift back to you. Take it. Open to it. Own it. It is yours.

"You ARE the goddess who walks on this earth. Remember this. Take back your gifts. You must no longer give them away. They are your birthright.

"Create. Nurture. Teach. Be in your beauty!

"In Lak Ech"

My Thoughts
Transmission I

When this transmission came through I was very excited. I felt I was in touch with an ancient matriarchal teaching that had profound implications. I had never thought of my womb as a place of creating anything other than a baby. I understood from my guidance that the womb is the microcosm of the macrocosm. The macrocosm is the great void from which everything is birthed. Our female body contains a womb, which gives us the potential for incredible creative power. Using the earth to birth our creation, we form a harmonious partnership with a most powerful deity, 'Gaia' or 'Mother Earth.'

I believe this is part of a matriarchal lineage teaching that has been buried for a long time. It is surfacing now to empower those of us who are ready to come into our true essence. This is an awakening for women of all ages. This also is important for women who have had their uterus removed — the energy of the uterus is still very much in place so the creative power has not been lost.

The deeper I delve into the mysteries, the better my understanding of why we as women have been oppressed for so long. There is no doubt that ages ago women as empowered, self-realized beings were a huge threat to the encroaching power of religious institutions that sought absolute control. Our intuition, our connection to nature, our partnership, and the honoring of plants, animals, cycles of the moon, etc., served us with wisdom and higher consciousness. Efforts by the church to suppress the teachings of the feminine mysteries have created a void in our awareness of the true power women possess.

The thought that my womb is a tool of endless possibilities and manifestations is enough to spark in me a new way of regarding my body. For my entire life I have lived under the notion that my body has functions that last a certain amount of time until my body ages and dies. Nowhere in my experience have I been taught that my body is magical. I'm now waking to the realization that my body is like a bio-computer. It is capable of tremendous power that can only begin to be accessed with the realization of its potential. We are told we only use 10% of our brain — 90% remains un-accessed. Perhaps as we awake to the untapped creative capability of our wombs we will open neural pathways in our brain. We will perhaps begin to think differently as we expand our perceptions of who we really are.

I did put this teaching into action after receiving it. At the time, I had been thinking about the 'evolved feminine.' This is the feminine in action who is not petty,

shallow, self-serving, or competitive with her sisters —
exactly the opposite of how much of our media portrays
women. Think all music videos, America's Top Model,
and reality TV shows.

The evolved feminine walks the path of beauty. She
regards herself and all life as sacred. She is sovereign unto
herself — she's not enslaved or anyone's fool. She relies
upon her intuition and wisdom. She is connected directly to Source and is aware of her connection to all things
above and below. She seeks the truth and embodies wisdom, healing, and service to the Divine. Expression and
expansion of the energies that honor all life are found
within her. This is the feminine I hope to see expressed
around the world. She is sorely needed at this time.

Setting an Intention

I decided that I would carry this evolved feminine in my
womb and birth her into my sacred circle in the woods.
My intention was to birth that energetic so it would be
available to women everywhere. I put my hands over my
womb and placed a seed of intention within me. I envi-
sioned this seed taking root and vowed to 'feed' it with
love and attention. Over the next couple of weeks I felt
like I was growing a beautiful gift. At night in bed I

would place my hands on my womb 'in adoration' as Ix Chel taught — sending in bright and nourishing light.

During one of my meditations around this time, I received a vision of a little green plant that looked bright and vigorous. I realized that the seed I'd planted within me was now a vibrant seedling. It felt healthy and joyful. I was surprised and delighted that it was communicating with me. This entire spiritual journey has been so wondrous because it is quite different from my earlier life experience. In the past, I only had snippets of sensitivity to the subtle realms, and now I am very much in tune with them. It's a wonderful feeling.

I marked on my calendar the day I would give birth and when the time came I went out to my circle to prepare. I had saved my menstrual blood in my 'moon bowl' and poured it out around the perimeter of the circle as a gift to Gaia. I called on the directions to send in their energies of support and I made more offerings of corn meal, chocolate, and incense. I found a perfect place on the ground where I squatted and focused on energetically birthing my gift into the earth. I was in a state of stillness and deep honoring.

I could feel a sensation of energy going from my vagina deep within the earth. I asked the Mayan grandmother, Ix Mukane, the keeper of the center of the earth, to receive my gift with all my love and gratitude for her support. I stayed like that for several minutes until I felt I had passed my entire offering into the earth. Then I waited as Ix Chel had instructed. A moment later I 'felt' a lush, green, vigorous vine growing up under me and enveloping my back and left side. It felt loving and sensual. It crept around to the front of my body and caressed my cheeks with its leaves. In that moment, I realized that this was Mother Earth reflecting back to me what I had just birthed. She had taken it and created this lovely vibrant vine of indescribable beauty. I was moved to tears. I felt the earth's gratitude for my integrity of purpose and I was deeply touched. It was a profound moment for me. My loving connection to Gaia was undeniable.

I feel like I am integrating this teaching and its implications more and more each day. The thought of thousands of awakened women on this planet doing this is exciting. Imagine the possibilities for great beauty that women could create — we all have the power to make this happen.

TRANSMISSION 2

Sacred Bathing

"Treat yourselves to the newness of discovery. For you do not truly understand the magic your body holds. It is in this connection to the magic that communion with Divine Love can occur. Light fills every cell in the body. Every cell is precious and a universe unto itself. Therefore, the body represents a cosmic temple — a place for the Divine to reside. Upkeep requires simple love and nurturing — qualities of the feminine that must be brought forward again.

"Conditioning through life has dulled the awareness of the brilliance your bodies contain. Disregard for the body has broken the feminine heart. Perceived flaws, misgivings, and self-hatred pervade the feminine consciousness, and illness finds a home in your shattered bodies. The key to your happiness on earth is revealed when you discover the magic your body carries.

"You are walking goddesses. Adorn yourselves. Take the time necessary to love your body. Feed the beauty that lives in you through the portal of ritual.

"Begin by engaging the water elemental. Draw a bath and infuse it with oils, with scent,

with salt from the sea. Bring in the fire elemental with candles. Lie in this bath and let the water draw out all your sorrows, all your hatred, all your fear. Feel the loving embrace of water holding your body, enveloping every inch in its healing fluid.

"Water makes no distinctions when it surrounds your body. No part of you is deemed unworthy of its caress. Meditate on this. The water takes in all of you. Every sacred inch of your flesh it caresses.

"Engage in conversation with the water elemental. She is a great healer and will offer you comfort and wisdom. Take the time necessary to create this ritual of self-love. Do this seven times between the full moons. A transformation will occur within you. Engagement with an ancient consciousness you all hold will develop over time.

"Through this simple offering to yourself you will open a chamber filled with memory. The water opens the inner doorways. Immerse your luscious, sensual, sacred bodies into her depths.

"In Lak Ech"

MY THOUGHTS
TRANSMISSION II

This piece came through and I must tell you that I am not a bath person. Up to that point I knew nothing of bathing rituals. So I did what I love to do in those situations, I went to Google. I looked for books on sacred bathing and found one called, *Spiritual Bathing: Healing Rituals and Traditions from Around the World,* by Rosita Arvigo and Nadine Epstein. This book is out of print but it called to me and I was able to order it from a used book source.

The day the book arrived, I opened the box, took out the book, and just 'happened' to open it to the page with the heading: 'Maya Sweat Lodges or Zumpulche.' Below was a paragraph on the purification rituals of Mayan sweat baths. I had one of those moments with the full body chill. I turned the page and there was a photograph of a cenote, which is an underground water hole. They are very beautiful and considered sacred to the Maya. I realized I had opened to the chapter in the book called, *The Maya: In Search of Spiritual Healing.* It is interesting that of all the chapters on various cultures, I would open to this one.

From the book I learned that spiritual bathing is still an important piece of the indigenous Maya medicinal practices. The Mayan people, adults and children alike, regularly bathe themselves in water that is infused with prayers, sacred herbs, and flowers. These carry a frequency that elevates the bath to a communion between the water elemental and the bather. The Mayans feel that this ensures their emotional, spiritual, and physical well-being.

Mayan baths address the diseases of the soul, known as spiritual disease. These could be depression, fear, grief, loneliness, etc. Mayan medicine men and women choose from different plants depending on the ailment and the symptoms. Each plant addresses a specific malaise. According to Arvigo, belladonna plants are used for insomnia or recurring nightmares — basil and rue aid in ridding the self of envy and jealousy.

These herbs are gathered ritualistically. Before they are picked, prayers of thanks, and intention are said to each plant. The number of plants used is also very important. Three, four, seven, and nine are sacred numbers to the Maya.

Incense is also a component to the sacred bath. It is understood that incense is a good ch'ulel carrier. Ch'ulel is vital energy that is necessary for the health of the soul. To the Maya, the gods have imbued each and every living thing with ch'ulel since the beginning of time. By lighting incense one bathes the energy body and the surrounding environment with ch'ulel. So the bath now becomes a source of clearing, healing, and strength.

To take seven baths I had to schedule them on my calendar as I would an appointment. Otherwise, it simply wouldn't happen. I'm afraid I can get caught up in the business of the day and a private ritual such as this can easily be put on the back burner. I was determined to put the teaching from Ix Chel into practice. I made these 'appointments' for myself and indulged in what became a sacred rite into a sea of tranquility.

I purchased sea salt and infused it with essential oils. If specific herbs are not available to pick, the next best thing is the essential oil of the plant, which carries potency unto itself. One can say a little prayer of thanks and intention to the deva of the plant oil. It is said that in the better essential oils, the deva of the plant is still present. My first bath was imbued with sea salt, infused with lavender and frankincense. I tuned in to my inner guidance and came up with these particular scents. Frankincense oil is said to promote spiritual awareness, clear negativity, and uplift the soul among other things. Lavender oil is balancing, calming, cleansing, and healing. The infusion smelled heavenly and I was ready to step into an oasis of quiet sanctuary.

For incense, I burned sandalwood, which filled the room with an intoxicating scent. Just the smell of good incense alone has a calming effect on me. I lit candles that surrounded the tub and also placed large, oval river rocks around the tub to bring in the grounding earth element. I had a vase of gorgeous flowers in the corner and the whole effect was temple-like. Having never approached a bath in this way before, the sacredness of what I had just created was not lost on me. I then spoke to the water, offering a prayer of gratitude and appreciation, and asking for a release of what no longer served me.

Stepping into the tub I instantly shifted. The scent, the candles, the beauty of my surroundings, and the warmth and feel of the water was a balm to my soul. Dear Goddess, why had I not given this gift to myself before? I had no idea. I stayed in that tub for half an hour, lost in myself, deeply relaxed, and gently caressed by the water. The experience was an act of self-love — an honoring of my beautiful body and my beautiful being within. I vowed then to make the time to do this regularly, certainly six more times before the next full moon.

Each subsequent bath had a special quality of its own. I learned to let painful emotions surface, which I then released into the water using its warm caress to fill me with nurturing love. These baths became a fertile ground of gentle healing and restorative energy for me. It was my secret escape and I came to treasure this time of self-love.

By the next full moon I had bathed seven times and I felt like a new person. There is a deeply felt internal shift that occurs when you honor yourself enough to create sacred ritual in honor of you. This is no small act and we do well to incorporate this into our busy lives. It is the realization that we are sacred, precious, powerful beings of indescribable beauty. In honoring ourselves through these rituals of self-love, we become precious and sacred to ourselves.

TRANSMISSION 3

Beauty

"*This is about beauty. The beauty you exude from within and the beauty you surround yourself with. My dears, the Goddess radiates great beauty everywhere she walks. Your piece is to create it all around you. The beauty of your heart is the first place you can start. Clear away the energies that cloud the light of your heart. Put your hands over your heart chakra and send healing, love, and laughter.*

"*Think of these as little house cleaners, going in to sweep away what doesn't have to be. Then feel the radiance beam out through your hands, filling the entire space with the beauty of your heart. In this way you have just created great beauty all around you and it came from your own heart. You can do this anywhere you are. If you are in a place that is ugly, or depressing, or scary, do this special thing. First clear around your heart and then beam it all around you. You will see that everything will change.*

"*For physical beauty I say to take time to create as much beauty as your world can take. Revel in your own beauty. Indulge in colors that* make you feel beautiful. Wear your jewelry if it nourishes you.

"You understand the essence of beauty. You are 'woman' and you are meant to express this gift. This is something to revel in. It is not the same as vanity. This is an expression of the divine beauty within you that seeks expression in everything you do. So, be in your beauty my daughters. Be unafraid and be bold!

"In Lak Ech"

MY THOUGHTS
TRANSMISSION III

Showering the earth with our beauty came in very powerfully for me. I was curious about the action of emanating the beauty energy of our heart into the environment. I am someone who likes to experiment so I decided to put this into practice.

Initially, I started the heart piece in my home office. After my morning meditation I put my hands over my heart chakra, sent in peace and joy, and then emanated outward a radiance of light from my heart. I focused on this for a few minutes and asked that the energy enhance the space for the rest of the day. About 15 minutes later, my youngest daughter awoke from sleep and came in to say good morning. After a hug and kiss she looked around my office and said, "I love this place!" She comes into my office to greet me every morning and what a nice bit of synchronicity that she would make that comment at that particular time.

In applying this simple practice out in the world, I realized as I went along that it required a clear focus of intent. I really understood the need to bring in the awareness of healing, love, and joy. When going about my day-to-day business I have a completely different mindset. So I began to take a moment or two to bring these energies into my heart that seemed to align me to wherever I felt a sense of 'center.' I would then radiate my heart's light.

Now I do this in my car when I remember. My children will attest to this — my general orneriness when driving has all but dissolved. What I found particularly interesting was that when I would remember to fill my car with my heart energy, my girls wouldn't bicker which they tended to do from time-to-time. That was an unexpected and most welcome side effect — so this has become a regular practice for me.

I would be curious to see what would happen if this was used with a large group of people — perhaps a large group visiting the White House or the United Nations. If one person can shift the energy of the space around them, imagine the power of several or hundreds or thousands of people gathering in a space and focusing on just this exercise. It seems so simple and I have a sense that it would be quite powerful.

As Ix Chel says, by radiating heart energy we create beauty all around us. Unfortunately we spend too much time criticizing ourselves. We hate our bodies. We seek ways in which to minimize, maximize, extrude, enhance, offset, and pretty much violate the integrity of our physicality. All this to mold ourselves into what we perceive to be 'beautiful' based on the whims of our culture.

Close the magazines, turn off the TV, and begin the art of self-love, which connects us with our inherent beauty. Through acts of kindness to ourselves, and attention paid to our lovely bodies and precious psyches, we deepen our connection to our beauty. We adorn ourselves with clothing that makes us feel beautiful. We wear jewelry that lights up our face and gives sparkle to our loving hands.

We wear make-up or not. We take private time to nurture ourselves through writing, meditation, walking in nature, or bathing, whatever it is that quickens us in our alone time.

Rethinking our bodies as vessels of radiance, wisdom, and joy rather than something that needs constant improvement, returns us to our truth. And that truth exudes great beauty that emanates from our eyes, our smiles, and the way we move. We are here to express this beauty, to share it with others, and to shower it upon the earth.

The Lakota people say their good-byes to each other with a comment, 'Walk in Beauty.' To walk in beauty is to be in a state of awareness that is best described as grace. This walk is to have beauty above, beauty below, and beauty on every side. It is the understanding that we are in perfect flow with the universe. In beauty we strive to be harmless to others and ourselves. To me, this is the beauty of the goddess. We are here to be in this beauty. To express this beauty. To walk in beauty.

As I Walk
with Beauty

As I walk, as I walk

The universe is walking with me

In beauty it walks before me

In beauty it walks behind me

In beauty it walks below me

In beauty it walks above me

Beauty is on every side

As I walk, I walk with Beauty.

Traditional Navajo Prayer

Spaciousness and Creating

"Creation isn't to be snuffed out.

"Listen to your inner guidance. Follow the leads that are given. You will always know what to do. Have absolute trust in the guidance that is handed to you through your own Divinity. This is freedom. To be aligned with your one true self —your connection to Source. You are forever. You are that which cannot be defined. You are that which cannot be held back or imprisoned. It is only through your perceptions of the limits that are in place that you can be enslaved to the constructs of your mind. But you are participating in a great play.

"Step back and expand until you cannot feel a sense of the confines of your body. Become space. All passes through you. Now you can see, know, and feel the ALL of Spirit. Leave the realm of ordinary senses and become the All of it. This is where you will find peace. The more often you do this, the better you become until you realize you can shift your reality completely.

"Now create what you want in alignment with divinity. Create from spaciousness — silence

and expansion is consciousness. Life will imitate the sacred and all will be infused with consciousness. Bring this forward. Become the great creatrix. Practice the art of becoming spaciousness. Go there often and bring back wisdom. It will come naturally because you are exposing yourself to consciousness. Connect to Source and you will receive the wisdom and the knowing of how to manifest a new earth.

"In Lak Ech"

MY THOUGHTS
TRANSMISSION IV

This transmission came through at a time when I was deep in fear about a host of depressing situations on the planet. We all have our triggers for fear. Whenever I explore the darker agenda of 'the new world order' I send myself into a labyrinth of fear.

We do live in three-dimensional reality and therefore a world of polarity — good/evil, dark/light, etc. And I know that ALL of it is divine. You can't appreciate the good without the bad, as they say, and we learn from adversity. Nevertheless, I still freak out with some of the information I read that is not found in the mainstream media.

For myself, I end up depressed for a bit and then I have to reconnect myself to Spirit by going within. My daily meditation practice allows me to sit in quietude and ponder the issue. Then I wait to see if something comes through. With my newfound ability to receive transmissions from Ix Chel, I tune in to her and ask for wisdom. Once again, Ix Chel is giving my power back to me through her teaching. I am in charge. I have access to clear guidance and I am a sacred, sovereign being.

Ix Chel said in her transmission, *"It is only through your perceptions of what limits are in place that you can be enslaved to the constructs of your own mind."* This is a huge piece. Perception or the power of belief is everything. All perception is a mental construct; completely fabricated by whatever belief system we have in place. In my mind there are severe limitations on my freedom by perceived 'powers that be' and I become enslaved to the mental construct of that belief. It affects my mood, my nervous system, my immune system, etc. As a result, I may become a warrior, or a healer, or a cynical bummer to everyone around me. The fact of the matter is that when I free myself of my belief systems, I am in truth, completely free.

There are times when I need to pause and take a look at the larger picture. Ix Chel suggests entering into spaciousness through quiet focus to access that picture. She suggests accessing a place of expansion in which there is room for everything, the bad and the good. Leave the place of fear, reaction, and resultant constriction to access a place of opening and trusting. This 'spaciousness' is a place to access wisdom and creativity. None of this is available to me when I'm in reaction and fear. It is only when I'm in the center of stillness that I experience clarity. I can then create my world while I'm held in the calm of expanded consciousness.

This is important because we create with our thoughts. Energy follows awareness, so what we pay attention to will grow. If I'm in fear, thinking about the 'bad guys' and the evil they're creating, I'm actually giving them enormous power. I'm also creating negative situations for myself out of that fear. By grounding myself in stillness and expanding my awareness, I am able to create a better world. When I'm in this state I am beyond the space of emotion and reaction. I just 'am.'

It's time to dream a new dream. We can only do that from a place of peace and wisdom from within.

I am not an airy-fairy, 'love and light' person. I have my dark moods like anyone else. Rather than allow them to rule me, I go there for a short time and allow myself to explore those depths. My goal is to pull up some gems from that place. I then begin my reconnection to the spacious calm within. After doing this for some time I can feel calm beckoning to me and it is a blissful peace that I relish when I fully go there.

In terms of creating a new world, it is far more effective to create from a place of higher awareness. Many millions of us have been praying for peace for years and still we see war and violence everywhere. We pray for harmony and we see so much disharmony. We ask that people become more attuned to the planet and take better care of it — yet pollution is now threatening to ruin this once pristine planet. What exactly are we doing wrong?

The problem is we are trying to create with our MINDS. We pray with our minds, we visualize with our minds, and we set intention through our minds. Creating with these mindsets brings forth an energy of opposites. Remember, we live in a world of polarity and the mind functions from a place of polarity. This is how it perceives everything. Our left-brain thinks rationally. It separates, it compares, and it puts things in order. One of my teachers, Brugh Joy used to say, "If you want peace, march for war." Meaning — *that which we desire will automatically produce its opposite.* The mind must create an opposite for each thing it desires. This is the nature of how the mind works.

To create from a place of non-duality, it is necessary to bypass the mind and work from a place of spaciousness and connection to Spirit. To get to this place of being connected to the All, I have two access points. Both are found in meditation. One is a practice of simple spaciousness, which can be practiced and mastered quickly. The other is a more elaborate practice of going deeply into the heart and creating from the heart center. Either one will enable you to consciously create from a place of non-duality.

To practice going into spaciousness, imagine yourself floating high in the sky. Think of the feeling you would have, floating above the earth looking down, up, and in all directions. Imagine yourself very small within the vastness of your surroundings. Sense that you are in limitless space. Now expand and become part of this limitless space. This does take practice. If this scenario feels unsafe or just too vast, you can put yourself within a large sphere. This way you have a sense of being protected. You can also envision yourself floating within the great dark 'Void of the Mother.'

This is my favorite way to meditate as it sends me very deeply into my right-brain awareness, which is connected to everything with no judgment or rational thought. It feels like pure peace to me.

The second meditation takes you deeply into the heart and requires an initial centering and connection to the earth and the sky. This is a meditation I found in a beautiful book called, *Dreaming the Maya Fifth Sun,* by Leonide Martin.

Breathe deeply and relax your mind. Imagine a beautiful place on earth where you would love to be. Feel or see every detail of this place. Know that it is a gift from Mother Earth and feel the love for this sacred place welling up inside you. When you are over-flowing with love, send it down into the earth. Shower her with your love and gratitude for the beauty and splendor of this place she has provided for you. Wait for a moment and then open to receive her love back.

Keep this connection to Mother Earth and bring your awareness to Father Sky. Imagine yourself swimming in the stars, gazing at the glory of the planets, the fire of the sun, and the magic of the Milky Way. Immerse yourself in this grandeur. Feel all the love you have for this exquisitely beautiful universe. Feel deeply into this love until your cup runneth over and then send your love up to Father Sky. Shower the cosmos with your love and then wait for a moment and open to receive his love.

You are connected to earth, your divine mother, and sky, your divine father — above and below. In you, Spirit and matter are joined. You are now the divine child. The cosmic forces are unified within you. This is a wondrous state of awareness.

When you feel ready, bring your awareness inside your head behind your eyes. Become aware of the hardness of the skull and the constant vibrations within the brain as neurotransmitters are fired. This vibration makes the sound of 'OM.' Make this sound and feel it vibrating inside your head.

Gently bring your awareness down through your throat, slipping effortlessly into your chest. Here you will float slightly left and drop down gently into your beating heart. Feel the contrast between the hardness of your skull, and the downy soft, gentle energy within your heart. You are inside the sacred space of your heart. Tune in to your heartbeat and be soothed by it. The vibration of the heart sounds like an 'Aah.' Make this sound as you settle deeply into your heart space.

You are now within your essence. This is the sacred space in your heart that you can access to receive great knowledge. You may ask any question or you may create an intention from this place. You will receive answers and bring back wisdom. Spend as much time here as you wish.

There is a secret chamber in the heart as well. To get here, use the power of intention. If you need assistance, ask for guidance and your intuition will lead you. In this secret chamber the vibration rises in pitch. This is the birthplace of all creation where the divine resides within you. This is the place where you can create from non-duality. Every possibility exists here. When you are ready, bring your awareness gently back to the rest of your body and slowly open your eyes.

Now you have learned how to co-create with the divine within you. This space of being-ness has no rationality, no logic. It creates through the symbolism of images and dreams. Here is the space where you can truly dream a new dream. It is a place of purity where your emotions and feelings create a beautiful world of unified consciousness.

We create everyday. These meditation modalities bring us to the place where we can create united with Source. This way we are coming from a place of infinite possibility not hindered by our rational thinking minds.

Radiance
of the Sun

"The properties of the sun's rays send codes and giftings into the receiver of the light. Look into the sun. Lift your face to its light. Illumine the entire span of your field with its rays. Allow your energy body to soak in this light then bring it into the physical body.

"Feel the sun's rays illuminating every cell. Envision the interior of your body aglow in red light as the blood pulses with sunlight coursing through your veins. See your bones filled with light. Feel into every bone throughout your body, beginning with the skull and working downward. Visualize the bones as light-filled to the point of blinding.

"Now notice the organs that are glowing with sunlight. Feel them warming to the point where they are lit with fiery light, burning off toxins and strengthening healthy cells. Know that inside your body, every part of you is aware of the sun. You were designed to bask in sunlight. Take it in deeply and feel its nourishment throughout the body.

"Different times of the day produce different hues of light, each with their own special proper-

ties. *The sun offers its gifts throughout the day and there are particular times when certain qualities are more accentuated. Early morning light has qualities of softness, nurturing, renewal, and joy — a good time to bring light within for healing emotional pain, depression, and apathy. It is also the light of dreams, hope, and excitement for what life will bring to a new day. As you receive its light, send to the sun your dreams. Now you have begun your dialogue with a most potent Spirit.*

"The midday sun has intensity, strength, and passion to it. Taken in for just minutes, it penetrates and burns away illness, anger, and resentments. The other piece to this is fuel for ideas, strengthening of will, and great fire for creative endeavors. This can be accessed throughout the bright of the afternoon.

"As the day wanes and the sun begins its descent, its light can penetrate the heart and heal the aches of love and loss. Then calm and clarity of mind can be accessed. The ability to let go brings new potentials after the restful, stillness of night.

"When the sun is not available to you, meditate on its golden rays and bring them to you.

"Align yourself with the great Spirit of the sun and it will find you always. You are a child of light. The sun is a great guide in this dimensional awareness. Awaken now to the technology of your body and the world of nature around you.

"In Lak Ech"

MY THOUGHTS
TRANSMISSION V

Before I began to experiment with what came through, I did a little digging into the cultures that worshiped the sun. There were numerous cultures throughout time that did so, regarding it as a God, Source, or Great Spirit. Native American cultures performed sun dances to honor its life-giving force. The ancient Egyptians worshiped the Sun God Ra. In India, devout Hindus begin their day at sunrise with a sun salutation called 'Surya Namaskar.'

There is a practice called sun gazing where one gazes into the sun either at sunrise or sunset when the rays are not as strong. It is an ancient practice of healing that originated in India 2600 years ago. Those who devote themselves to this practice experience a decrease in negative emotions like anger and depression. They feel an increased sense of calm and inner peace, along with strengthened immunity. Some have even healed disease with this practice.

In this transmission, Ix Chel does not discuss gazing into the sun so much as using the rays as a natural technology of nature that is readily available to us. I have practiced this as a form of meditation — I sit in the sunshine with my eyes closed and my mind focused on bringing the rays inward. It is a powerful meditation to do as one can feel a physical sensation of energy throughout the body. I believe we can affect healing through this one practice.

It is understood that the sun stimulates our serotonin levels in the brain which affects our mental health and well-being. The sun also stimulates endorphin levels and has natural antibacterial properties that help skin disorders like acne and eczema. In addition, we make 90% of natural Vitamin D in our body through exposing it to the sun, which has pronounced healing effects for some cancers.

These results are from simply exposing oneself to the sun for a period of time. With this practice, we are doing more by directing the rays inward through conscious focus. My teacher, Tom Kenyon, always says, 'energy follows awareness.' Regrettably, we are aware of so little that goes on around us. We engage our five senses but our awareness of the more subtle realms that exist is pretty much non-existent. If we can step out of our standard perception of the sun's rays and expand our awareness of what those rays might be carrying, we would be able to utilize them more fully.

I have been sitting in the sun regularly, consciously bringing the rays inward and directing them to specific parts of my body. I do this for about 15 minutes. When I finish I am just buzzing with energy. My mind feels clear and I have a wonderful feeling of confidence when I'm done.

I sense there is mastery to this that comes with practice. I understand that I'm working with a powerful deity and it feels like a co-creative endeavor, which is empowering. I'm clearly on to something because I feel a sense of clarity and health whenever I do this and it lasts the entire day. I should also say that meditating daily helps with shifting states of consciousness.

This requires practice to get to a receptive state and feel the energy from this exercise.

My health and well-being is ultimately in my hands. As I grow closer to nature around me and engage it rather than simply cohabitate with it, I feel my awareness expanding. I'm discovering that nature communicates with us when we open and make ourselves available to it. And nature has much to teach us in the way of healing.

Cultures of old understood that the qualities of the sun were different depending on the time of day. Ancient Persian cultures worshiped the rising sun. Certain cultures like the Japanese had customs that were done at specific times of the sun's placement. One can easily feel the difference between the morning sunlight and the intense energy of the afternoon rays. The location of the sun in the sky determines certain qualities that are felt just by walking outside.

Early morning sun feels hopeful. It brings the promise and potential of a new beginning. I see the sun rising from my kitchen window in the morning and I have found myself stepping outside on my deck to give it a silent greeting. Then I send it my dreams for the day. This takes but a minute, yet it gives me a feeling of strong connection to my world. To sit for a few minutes and focus on this rising ball of exquisite beauty is indeed a balm for the soul. There is tremendous hope brought forth with the rising of the sun.

The idea of tuning in to the sun's rays at specific times of the day depending on what we want to manifest or let go of is yet another brilliant bit of creativity at our disposal.

If only we took the time to tune in to this. The sun and its glorious energy loom brightly above us. Clearly the ancient cultures understood its power to affect all of life on the planet on many levels. No doubt, many more than we consider today.

Living in Seattle, the sun is not so available in the colder months. I find myself longing to feel its warmth on my face and to walk on the warm ground.

To meditate for a short time and align with the great Spirit of the sun is an effective way to raise my Spirits. It's about tuning in, becoming present and connecting to the energetic bandwidth of 'sun.' One can tune in and visualize these rays penetrating the entire body, filling it with warmth and light. I have done this in the early morning hours in my meditation practice and it carries me through the day.

Always remember that energy follows awareness. Focus and visualization brings this energy into the body and it will respond with a sense of well-being. Healing on many levels is possible with continued practice and focus.

TRANSMISSION 6

Path of the Heart

"The pathway is open to you, it leads to your heart. There are many treasures to be found here. In this time of chaos and upheaval, the first treasure awaiting you is forgiveness. It is imperative for your development that you forgive those who have forgotten their divinity and seek to diminish those they deem inferior. It is but a perspective and they too have the ability to see their way out of it. You must not doubt the divinity within them.

"At the same time, do not make a slave of yourself. You must forgive to be free and you must also exercise wise discernment. As you move further along this path to the heart, you will be asked to conduct yourself with impeccability. Speak only the truth despite your fears. Be a light to those who seek it and leave the rest alone. They will come around in time.

"Spend more of your time away from the diversions of your culture and commune deeply with your land. You are of it and it will respond to your sincere attention. Come to it for counsel — the trees, the plant Spirits, the animal Spirits, and the elementals. They will welcome

you to an etheric table of enlightened discussion.

"Put your hands on the ground and send your intention into me. I will respond. My words may be expressed differently but you will always understand.

"The more you offer honoring to Mother Earth, the more wisdom you will receive. In situations of confusion or uncertainty, you will know what to do. When healing is needed, you will bring through the balm. Walk gently on the earth and practice stillness so I may come to you.

"The path of the heart is golden. Spirit in all things becomes ever more obvious and ever more available as you walk this path.

"In Lak Ech"

MY THOUGHTS
TRANSMISSION VI

When I think of the path to the heart, it makes perfect sense to me that you cannot get there without the ability to forgive. In the heart there is room for 'the whole, the All of it.' Everything is sacred when viewed from the heart space. One cannot connect to it deeply if there is any kind of preference regarding what is good and what is considered to be not good. So, if we are carrying anger or resentment toward others we certainly cannot fully access this space.

To withhold forgiveness means to carry an extra psychic load. This often leads to an eventual manifestation of illness or misfortune. It is a heavy weight to carry and it certainly doesn't contribute to personal happiness. To honestly recognize the divinity within each of us, regardless of our surface judgments, is a step closer to the space of the heart.

The thought that kept coming to me regarding this piece is "clean up your past.' I have felt the call to let go of the resentments I have been carrying over the years for various slights, hurts, and injustices I have endured by whomever. At the same time, I feel understandable outrage at the abuses of power I see going on around on our planet today.

To see the divinity in the people carrying out these abuses is a huge challenge for me. However, when I can calm and center from my heart, I get a sense that we are all part of a grand play. Some of us have come here to play the so-called 'good guys' and some of us agreed to play the 'bad guys.' Viewed from this larger awareness, I am able to glimpse the divinity within these people. At the same time it doesn't stop my activism, but it surely tempers my reaction.

In regard to behaving with impeccability, I am reminded of a healing session I had with a client. I felt the presence of her deceased father come into me and I opened myself to receive any message he might have for his daughter. When the session was over I began to tell my client what happened. I then saw her eyes fill with anticipation, tears, grief, and hope. It was one of those moments when I realized the full weight of the responsibility that comes with the deepened sensitivity I've developed along the spiritual path. I realized how easy it would be to manipulate someone who is trusting and vulnerable. And it humbled me greatly and enhanced my sense of compassion and honoring for the people who come to me for help.

Ego is a necessary piece to address on the spiritual path. It is as common among spiritual teachers as it is among doctors, politicians, lawyers, etc. Part of this work is to clean up our own backyard through addressing our shadow aspects, the parts of ourselves we've cast out.

We cannot be a light to others when we are lacking awareness about our personal selves. As someone who is far from perfect (and in excellent company I'm sure), I do make a practice of keeping a watchful eye on the various parts of myself that like to get all puffed up and important when they feel 'special.' Not that we can't feel special. I'm talking here about that feeling of 'I've got something you don't.' It is my ego's way of separating itself and there is always that tendency to feel kind of superior, in a way, if I'm not conscious.

Truly walking in impeccability is to know yourself so completely that you can recognize yourself in everyone. This is where the connection, the feeling of oneness, the desire to commune is more important than judging. This is the place from where I can speak my truth and recognize where it will be heard and welcomed.

Communion with the natural world around me has become a vital component to my sense of self. Spending time in the woods just listening to the birds, and the sound of the wind through the trees grounds and centers me. And I find myself going to that place for 'counsel' often. I focus on simply sending my love and gratitude into the earth while I sit in my quiet space.

In doing this, I have deepened my sense of connection to Mother Earth and the Spirits around me. Despite the various events that go on in the world, I find that I can calm myself when I go into my back woods and just 'be.' Looking at these transmissions, I see a consistent message of honoring the body and communing/communicating with the earth. It is easy to lose that sense of connection in our modern, busy world. And yet without it, we are unconscious.

To many there is a sense that something is missing, and if we stay busy and entertained enough we won't have to think about it. I sometimes wonder if we're not quite mature enough to handle all of this technological wizardry.

Sitting in front of a screen all day and/or through the night isn't going to offer what nature gives us so lovingly — a sense of sacred purpose and belonging to this earth.

I did a ceremony yesterday where I sat in my sacred circle in my back woods and drummed and sang to the earth, the sky, and the four directions. It was a simple ceremony and yet I felt more connected to those energies than I have ever felt. My circle was pulsing with Spirit energies and I could still feel them around me as I wrote this piece. I understand that through my offering I receive great gifts from Spirit. True wisdom is birthed within through connection and appreciation of the land.

This I know.

TRANSMISSION 7

Sacred Blood

"The womb is a sacred container. Within this container is produced the moon blood that represents both life and death. The release of this blood brings forth the opportunity to make a powerful offering to Mother Earth. Sacred 'itz' is in this blood and whether or not you choose to make a formal offering, it is beneficial for you to be conscious of the energy your moon blood carries.

"Do not shy away from your blood. Look at it. Explore its mystery. What might it be trying to tell you? Look at the color. What does it smell like? Your blood can indicate the health of your body and it can warn you of illness. It is potent food for the soil and the very act of you offering it honors all life.

"Allow yourself to go within during your bleeding. Listen for the voices of your ancestors. Call on them to teach you the sacred wisdom of the moon time. You were once revered for having the ability to bleed in this way. Call back the honoring, the heartfelt respect, and the reverence that women felt for each other and themselves.

"Draw to you sisters who will gather with you during this time. In your modern world the sacred lodges and temples of the blood time may not be feasible as yet. Call your sisters and gather for but a few hours to share.

"The potency of expression during this time is a gift. When you still yourself and calm the momentum of your daily life, the emotions that come through can be most illuminating. You must honor the authentic feelings you bring through at this time and stop diminishing them. They seek expression and you must give yourself a place to bring them forward.

"A journal serves as a sacred accounting of the truth you express. I invite you to go into nature and pour out your soul's expression. Squat down and put your hands on the earth and send the emotions you wish to unleash. Shed your tears, spill your frustrations, and whisper your desires. This time of heightened emotions has great value. Give your emotions voice. And if you feel so inclined, bleed directly onto the earth and feel into the sacredness of this act.

"You bring forward new life through child-birth — and through the potent offering of your *blood that feeds the earth and stimulates the growth of life-giving plants. Your power is immense. Shed the layers of lies you have been told and birth the age of woman remembered.*

"In Lak Ech"

MY THOUGHTS
TRANSMISSION VII

I was happy when this teaching came through. I wanted Ix Chel's teaching on the moon time so I could share it with the women at the full moon ceremonies. Since that transmission I have plunged myself deeply into the blood mysteries.

At the onset of my menarche there was no celebration. There was no meaningful ritual of any kind. I was handed a sanitary pad with a belt that attached to it and told how to use it. My mother wasn't taught about the sacredness of women's bleeding, nor was her mother, or her mother's mother. I grew up Irish Catholic and the shame and suppression around menstruation was everywhere I looked.

Eventually, my period became a monthly inconvenience for me. I dreaded it and I just wanted it to be over. I had a healthy distrust for pharmaceuticals so I never went on the pill. Many of my friends did take the pill — not only for birth control but to reign in their periods.

I never came across any books or information about the blood mysteries until recently. At the age of 46, I am most grateful that I still have a few years left to truly appreciate my moon time.

When I was 40 at the advice of my gynecologist, I began using an IUD. Normally, I would have run screaming at the very thought of doing something like this but I trusted her and she told me they were safe. She also told me that because I was so athletic, I probably wouldn't bleed with the IUD. That got my attention and I jumped at the chance to not have to deal with my period.

For three years I had no period. During the third year of wearing the IUD I began mystery school training with one of my spiritual teachers, Dr. Brugh Joy. It was in-depth, psycho-spiritual work and as the year progressed I began to feel that I needed to be bleeding monthly. This came to me as an intuitive hit and it haunted me until I finally made an appointment with my gynecologist to have the IUD removed.

The weekend before that appointment I flew to Arizona for a five-day retreat with Brugh. We were working with shadow material, integrating the cast-out parts of ourselves that we project onto others. During one of the sessions, Brugh called me on a shadow piece I carried unconsciously. Of course, this was mortifying to my ego. I was up most of the night endeavoring to integrate and accept that part of myself.

The following day, I was shown a vision of myself as a character, in my life, where I exhibited the very qualities of the shadow piece that I had been projecting onto others. There was no feeling of judgment in this vision — it was a gift. I was simply shown instances where I behaved in the ways that I abhorred in others. It was uncovered in such a loving way that I instantly got the larger picture and saw this piece as a clump of trees in my forest of being. It didn't define me but it was part of me nonetheless.

I went into the morning's session and shared this realization and felt an intense shift in my psyche. When the lunch break came, I began having stomach cramps. I went to the bathroom and discovered I was bleeding. Another gift had come my way. At that moment, there was no way I could adequately express the gratitude I felt. I then vowed to honor my cycle and treat my female functions with respect and appreciation.

I flew home the following day and my flow was particularly heavy. I had horrendous cramping which did not feel like normal menstrual pain. Something inside my womb was hurting and I couldn't figure out what was happening. That night I took a shower and felt something in my vagina and as I felt for it I realized the IUD had fallen into my hand. I knew instantly that the shift I experienced at the retreat had released the IUD.

I called my gynecologist and was put on the phone with one of those people who is on call over the weekend and was clearly at the end of her 24-hour call duty. She was curt and irritated and I found myself apologizing for disturbing her. I told her my IUD came out in the shower and she said, "That's not possible. It can come out in the first couple of months but not after three years."

"Well, I'm holding it in my hand and it came out on its own." I replied.

She told me to come in first thing Monday to be checked and said again, "That is very unusual — that shouldn't happen." That was confirmation that it was a result of the inner shift I had experienced at the retreat.

The following day, I took time to sit in my meditation room. I lit a candle and put my hands on my womb. And with sincerity said, "I am so sorry. I didn't know. I didn't know how sacred you were. Nobody told me and I have been completely unconscious. I apologize from the bottom of my heart. I promise that I will open to what you want to teach me. I promise that I will honor my period and deepen my appreciation of its mystery. Thank you for being patient with me. Please heal and let me love you."

This was an elemental moment for me as I realized I had been damaging my body by not allowing it to flow in the instinctive way that female bodies have been flowing forever. I prayed I could reverse whatever damage I had done to myself physically, hormonally, and psychically.

Since then, I have incorporated the blood mysteries into my full moon ceremonies. Additionally, I have put together a separate monthly gathering just for moon time discussion and I teach a class on the blood mysteries. And to my two young daughters, I promise you will receive a beautiful initiation into your moon time.

I feel this is an area of importance for women to embrace. It is imperative that we honor the sanctity of our moon time for the sake of our younger sisters who are hungry for initiation and sacred purpose. I have listed a number of excellent books and websites on this topic under 'Helpful Books and Websites.'

Reflections on the Teachings of Ix Chel

In my meditations when I tune in to Ix Chel, I have asked her about the underlying message of many of her transmissions that reveal the magic of the body and the untapped power we possess. I have come away with a deeper understanding of the Human/Spirit experience.

We lost touch with the vast capabilities of our awareness ages ago. Over the past 2000 years or more, we've been assimilated into a belief system that separates the Spirit from the body. The body has been regarded as sinful, as lesser compared to the lofty realms of Spirit. Some think the body is something to be transcended. The fact is there is light in matter, which gives us enormous potential to develop all manner of abilities in the areas of healing, growth, and manifestation.

We are all a part of the great dance of life. We are like cells in a body. We are connected to each other as well as to every plant, animal, insect, bacteria, and particle of the cosmos. This means that our bodies are infused with that universal life force and everything is possible. Knowing this, we can use our bodies as vehicles to bring about incredible change both within and without.

There is much information available about this in the form of books and film such as, *What the Bleep, The Secret,* and the Abraham Hicks books, etc. Our world problems and our personal problems may seem daunting. The biggest secret is that not only do we have the power to shift our reality; we have the authority to do so. Ix Chel says that the time is now to reconnect directly to Source, God, the Creator. The time is now to take back our beautiful Mother Earth and birth a new reality where we as conscious humans create a world of peace and joy, for the planet and ourselves.

Now is the time to be BIG. If enough of us claim the power we have always carried, and use it in a way that honors life, our entire world will change. As divine creators, we must go from prayers of supplication and begging to a dialogue of POWER where our engagement with God is DIRECT. This is not a power that suppresses, grabs, and hordes. This is a true power, which carries with it the greatest reverence and respect. Creating from this place brings forth true grace. With this power, we can reverse suffering on all levels.

We have the ability to reach a level of illumination that can serve all of humankind. This is why the full moon ceremonies are so important to me. As women, we gather and inspire each other through the unimaginable power we all possess — to affect change. Using our own power in conjunction with the planetary energies, such as the moon's fullness, enables us to bring forth our vision in a co-creative way. We are in alignment with the universe and we use its energies to bring forth a new reality.

This journey I have undertaken has been wondrous and empowering. As I tune in to the Spirit of Ix Chel, who I perceive to be one of many divine messengers, I am opened more to the mystery of my own divine essence. It is a wondrous opportunity to be alive in a time of unprecedented expansion of consciousness. We are creating this shift together. May we all remember the true beauty of who we are and recognize that beauty in others. May we carry that vision of beauty into a future world of awakened, wise, and conscious beings who walk the path of the heart.

"In Lak Ech"

About the Author

Shamanic Therapist, Author, Teacher, Poet. Of Celtic heritage, Shonagh Home follows the wisdom of the ancients and serves as a Bàn Draoi (dree), and fili, which is Gaelic for a Celtic medicine woman/seer/poet. As a modern medicine woman, she brings her connection to nature and the spirit worlds into her flourishing practice, hosting retreats and working psycho-spiritually with clients from all over the world. She specializes in shadow work, delving into the rich territory of the psyche. In addition, Shonagh hosts The Mushroom's Apprentice podcast.

www.themushroomsapprentice.com
www.shonaghhome.com

Helpful Books and Websites

Books

Sastun by Rosita Arvigo

Rainforest Home Remedies by Rosita Arvigo

Herbal Healing for Women by Rosemary Gladstar

Healing Wise by Susun S. Weed

Dreaming the Maya Fifth Sun by Leonide Martin

Her Blood is Gold by Lara Owen

First Moon by Maureen Theresa Smith

Becoming Peers by DeAnna L'am

Songs of Bleeding by Spider

This is Who I Am by Rosanne Olson

The Woman in the Shaman's Body
by Barbara Tedlock, Ph.D.

WEBSITES

www.shonaghhome.com

www.casakin.com

www.rositaarvigo.com

www.arvigotherapy.com

www.susunweed.com

www.beheavenonearth.com